Built to Survive
NATURAL DISASTERS

THIS EDITION
Editorial Management by Oriel Square
Produced for DK by WonderLab Group LLC
Jennifer Emmett, Erica Green, Kate Hale, *Founders*

Editors Grace Hill Smith, Libby Romero, Maya Myers, Michaela Weglinski;
Photography Editors Kelley Miller, Annette Kiesow, Nicole di Mella; **Managing Editor** Rachel Houghton;
Designers Project Design Company; **Researcher** Michelle Harris; **Copy Editor** Lori Merritt;
Indexer Connie Binder; **Proofreader** Larry Shea; **Reading Specialist** Dr. Jennifer Albro;
Curriculum Specialist Elaine Larson

Published in the United States by DK Publishing
1745 Broadway, 20th Floor, New York, NY 10019

Copyright © 2023 Dorling Kindersley Limited
DK, a Division of Penguin Random House LLC
23 24 25 26 10 9 8 7 6 5 4 3 2 1
001-334084-July/2023

All rights reserved.

Without limiting the rights under the copyright reserved above, no part of this publication may be reproduced, stored in or introduced into a retrieval system, or transmitted, in any form, or by any means (electronic, mechanical, photocopying, recording, or otherwise), without the prior written permission of the copyright owner.
Published in Great Britain by Dorling Kindersley Limited

A catalog record for this book
is available from the Library of Congress.
HC ISBN: 978-0-7440-7435-2
PB ISBN: 978-0-7440-7436-9

DK books are available at special discounts when purchased in bulk for sales promotions, premiums, fundraising, or educational use. For details, contact: DK Publishing Special Markets,
1745 Broadway, 20th Floor, New York, NY 10019
SpecialSales@dk.com

Printed and bound in China

The publisher would like to thank the following for their kind permission to reproduce their images:
a=above; c=center; b=below; l=left; r=right; t=top; b/g=background

Alamy Stock Photo: Aflo Co. Ltd. / Nippon News / Rodrigo Reyes Marin 34, Yvette Cardozo 39t, Brandon Moser 24-25t, Reuters / Steve Nesius 26b, Joern Sackermann 30-31t; **Dreamstime.com:** 1000words 44-45, Aoldman 36bl, Andrii Biletskyi 28t, Boggy 17t, Chernetskiy 29, Andrey Dakutko 42cr, Danciaba 38b, Elwynn 20-21, F11photo 15br, Heike Falkenberg / Dslrpix 41tl, Michael Flippo 12cl, Martin Haas 8-9bc, Haywiremedia 37, Robert Lerich 11t, Wayne Mckown 19bl, Felix Mizioznikov 27cr, Sean Pavone 14, Stephan Pietzko 42cla, Oleksandr Rado 8bl, Raytags 12br, Dan Ross 9, Saiko3p 18t, Kathryn Sidenstricker 10t, Joe Sohm 42-43t, Jeff Stein 6-7, Enrique Gomez Tamez 19tr, Tokarsky 3cb, Topdeq 18tl, Paul Topp / Nalukai 33br, Yusa48 43cr, Alessandro Zappalorto 4-5, Zenobillis 22br; **Getty Images:** JIJI PRESS / AFP 32, The Image Bank / Gaylon Wampler 40-41, Stringer / ICON / AFP 1b; **Getty Images / iStock:** sshepard 13t; **Shutterstock.com:** FotoKina 23, Sunwand24 21cra, yevgeniy11 41cra; TCF Architecture / Eckert Architectural Photography: 35tr, 35c

Cover images: *Front:* **Shutterstock.com:** ollirg; *Back:* **Shutterstock.com:** VectorShow clb, YummyBuum cla

All other images © Dorling Kindersley
For more information see: www.dkimages.com

For the curious
www.dk.com

Level 3

Built to Survive
NATURAL DISASTERS

Libby Romero

Contents

- **6**   Building for Natural Disasters
- **8**   Tornadoes
- **15**   Earthquakes
- **22**   Hurricanes
- **28**   Floods
- **33**   Tsunamis

36 Blizzards
40 Wildfires
46 Glossary
47 Index
48 Quiz

Building for Natural Disasters

Some days are just perfect. Not too hot, not too cold—just right. On these days, nature can be a dream come true. But nature has a dangerous side, too. It can cause all sorts of natural disasters. Natural disasters can cause severe damage to the places where people live and work.

Fortunately, we have learned how to prepare for these events. And one thing we've learned is how to create strong buildings. Buildings can be designed to survive all sorts of natural disasters.

Tornadoes

A tornado is one type of natural disaster. Tornadoes are vertical funnels of rapidly spinning air. They form during some severe thunderstorms. A tornado can be more than a mile wide. Its winds can swirl over 200 miles per hour (322 kph). It can travel for many miles, destroying everything in its path.

To limit the damage from tornadoes, engineers have come up with some smart designs for tornado-resistant homes and buildings.

Finding Shelter
During a tornado, the safest places to be are underground, in a basement, or in an interior room with no windows.

Even weak tornadoes can damage square buildings with straight walls. When strong winds blow on a building with square corners, pressure builds up on one side. That makes the building more likely to collapse.

But what if the building is round? When strong winds blow across a dome, air pressure is evenly distributed across the entire building. That makes round buildings stronger. Their roofs, constructed with spokes like a wheel, are less likely to blow off, too.

Square buildings are more resistant to tornadoes if they're built out of strong materials. Steel is strong. So is concrete. Homes made of lumber and plywood can be reinforced so they are stronger, too.

plywood

steel

concrete

Some communities in areas that have lots of tornadoes have built safe rooms. These structures are built above the ground. But they are made out of materials like solid steel, so they can withstand tornado-force winds. The shelters have space for many people. They are a safe place to be if a tornado is approaching.

Earthquakes

During an earthquake, the ground shakes back and forth. Sometimes, it rolls like waves on an ocean.

Many buildings crack and crumble during an earthquake. So, it may seem unlikely that really tall buildings like skyscrapers would be able to resist such force. But they can!

Lots of the tallest skyscrapers are built in places that have earthquakes. Architects have found ways to make the buildings flexible. Because the buildings can bend, they're still standing when the swaying stops.

Holding Steady
No building is earthquake proof. The goal is to create buildings that are earthquake resistant.

The first step toward earthquake resistance starts deep in the ground. The Transamerica Pyramid in San Francisco, California, USA, was built in the 1970s. Its deep foundation is made of concrete and steel. During a really big earthquake, the top of the building sways—more than a foot in either direction! But the building is strong. It stays standing.

Solid Ground
Buildings that stand on solid bedrock shake less than those built on loose soil, sand, or reclaimed land.

Some newer buildings are built on top of flexible pads. The Yokohama Landmark Tower in Japan is built on top of rollers. Pads and rollers are made of flexible materials that sit between a building and its foundation. When an earthquake strikes, they absorb the vibrations. As the ground shakes, the foundation can move without moving the structure above it.

The Burj Khalifa in Dubai, UAE, is an extremely tall building. It has a strong base. It also has a network of cross-bracing steel beams and reinforced panels inside its walls. This framework turns the skyscraper into a stiff rod. That makes the building hold steady during an earthquake.

Strong and Flexible
Steel can be shaped so that it bends under stress instead of breaking.

This skyscraper also has a perimeter of columns on its outside walls. The columns connect to the inside walls. If an outer wall falls, the columns hold the inner walls in place. Anchors buried deep in the sand also help keep the building steady.

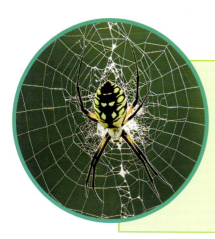

Nature's Builders
Pound for pound, spiderwebs are stronger than steel. Engineers study them for ideas about how to make stronger, more flexible building materials.

19

Earthquakes aren't the only thing that can make a skyscraper move. Strong winds can make the top floors sway back and forth, too.

To counter that movement, Taipei 101 in Taiwan has a giant pendulum between its 87th and 92nd floors. When the building moves, the pendulum swings in the opposite direction. This helps keep the skyscraper balanced.

Sharing Ideas
The same ideas that make skyscrapers strong can also protect smaller buildings during earthquakes.

Hurricanes

Hurricanes are one of nature's most powerful kinds of storms. They bring strong winds, heavy rainfall, storm surge, and flooding.

Because of the widespread damage they cause, hurricanes are one of the costliest weather disasters. And with climate change, hurricanes are becoming stronger. It's important for homes and buildings in hurricane-prone areas to be prepared.

Hurricane Watch
The official Atlantic hurricane season is from June 1 to November 30 each year.

The Eye of the Storm is a home located on Sullivan's Island, near Charleston, South Carolina, USA. It has survived several hurricanes.

This dome-shaped home is made of concrete and steel. Thick pilings anchor it to the ground. The home is shaped like an egg, so wind blows around it rather than straight into its sides.

All the living quarters are on the second and third floors—out of reach from rising waters. The ground level is used for parking and storage. There are also eight huge openings at the bottom of the home. When storm surge reaches the house, water moves through those openings. The home remains intact.

Not many people have dome-shaped homes. But most buildings can be made more resistant to hurricane damage thanks to some creative products.

Windows are a good place to start. Hurricane windows are similar to car windshields. They are made out of layers of laminated glass. This makes the windows flexible when strong winds blow. It also keeps them from shattering if they break.

Concrete is a good building material to use in a hurricane zone. Ultra-high performance concrete (UHPC) is even better. It is much stronger than regular concrete, lasts a lot longer, and can be made out of recycled materials. UHPC was first developed by the US Army for making nuclear blast shelters.

Surviving Irma
The Pérez Art Museum in Miami, Florida, USA, is made of ultra-high performance concrete. In 2017, it wasn't damaged at all when Hurricane Irma hit the coast as a Category 4 storm.

Floods

Howling winds may make the most noise during a hurricane. But storm surge causes the most damage. As the water level of the ocean rises, vast areas along the coast are flooded.

Many people live near the ocean. Lots of people live next to rivers, too. Rivers can overflow when there is too much rain.

One way to protect buildings from rising waters is to lift them above the waterline. Around the world, lots of buildings near water sit up on stilts. When the water level rises, the buildings are high enough to avoid being flooded.

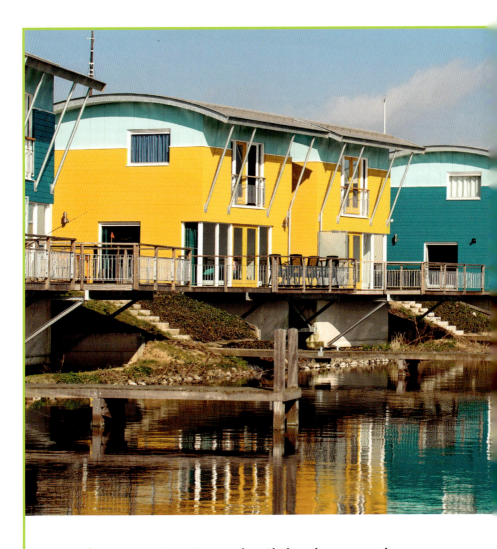

Another option is to build a home that floats—or at least one that floats whenever the water rises!

In the Netherlands, some houses are amphibious. Like frogs and toads, they can survive on land and in the water.

Water World
Flooding is a common problem in the Netherlands. About half of the country is at or below sea level.

Most of the time, the homes sit on concrete foundations—just like normal houses. But when the water level rises, the homes float on top of the water like boats. When the water goes back down, the houses do, too. The homes are attached to steel posts so they don't float away.

Tsunamis

Tsunamis are a different kind of flood. They occur when powerful earthquakes or volcanic eruptions rock the ocean floor. The shock triggers waves that travel across the ocean's surface. As the waves reach shallower water, they can swell to over 100 feet (30.5 m) high. They can travel more than a mile (1.6 km) beyond the shoreline.

If you can see a tsunami wave approaching, you won't have time to outrun it. It's time to seek shelter—as high up as you can get.

Speedy Waves
In the deep ocean, tsunamis travel over 500 miles per hour (800 kph).

Vertical tsunami shelters can keep you safe. They're sturdy enough to withstand the water's pressure. They are tall enough to keep you out of its reach. And they're big enough to give lots of people a place to escape from the rushing water.

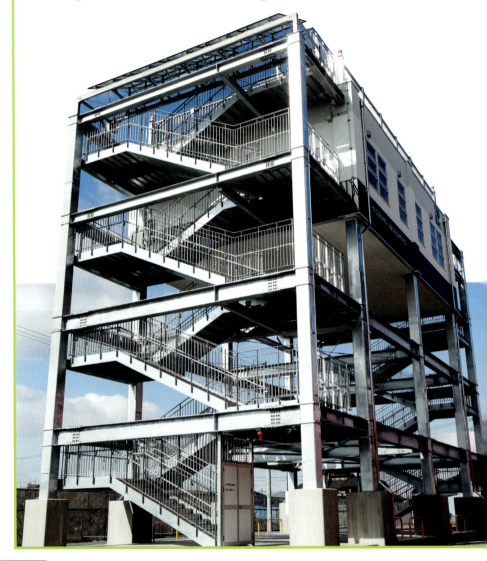

The gymnasium at Ocosta Elementary School in Westport, Washington, USA, is a tsunami evacuation structure. Around 1,000 people can fit on its roof.

Blizzards

For people living in colder climates, a blizzard is the storm to watch out for.

During a blizzard, the temperature drops below freezing. Huge amounts of snow fall from the sky. The wind howls, blowing at speeds greater than 35 miles per hour (56 kph). It's impossible to see very far. And all of this goes on for hours. Sometimes, it lasts for days.

For a building to withstand a blizzard, it must have a strong roof. Why? During a blizzard, snow piles up on top of the roof. And snow can be very heavy!

Heavy Loads
One foot of fresh snow weighs as much as three to five inches (7.6 to 12.7 cm) of packed snow or one inch (2.5 cm) of ice.

Dome-shaped buildings hold steady during blizzards for the same reason they can resist tornadoes. They can handle a lot of pressure. That means they can hold a heavy load of snow. But the snow might just slide off the round building instead.

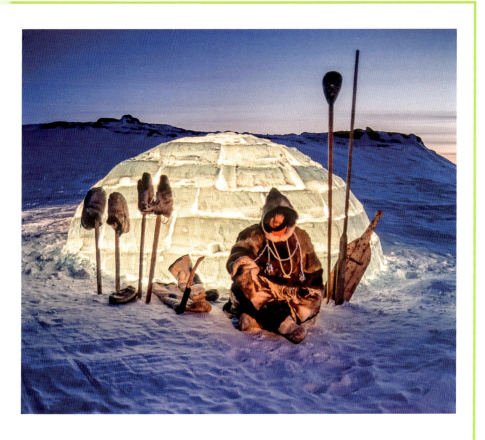

For temporary shelters, Inuit people sometimes build traditional dome-shaped igloos out of blocks of snow. A correctly built igloo is warm on the inside. It is strong enough on the outside to support the weight of a full-grown person. Igloos help people survive in cold northern climates—even through blizzards.

Wildfires

Wildfires can burn out of control in forests, grasslands, and prairies. Sometimes, they start naturally. Lightning strikes cause lots of wildfires. Sometimes, people start them. For instance, campers may not do a good job of putting out their campfire.

Regardless of how they start, wildfires can spread quickly. And they can burn whole communities to the ground.

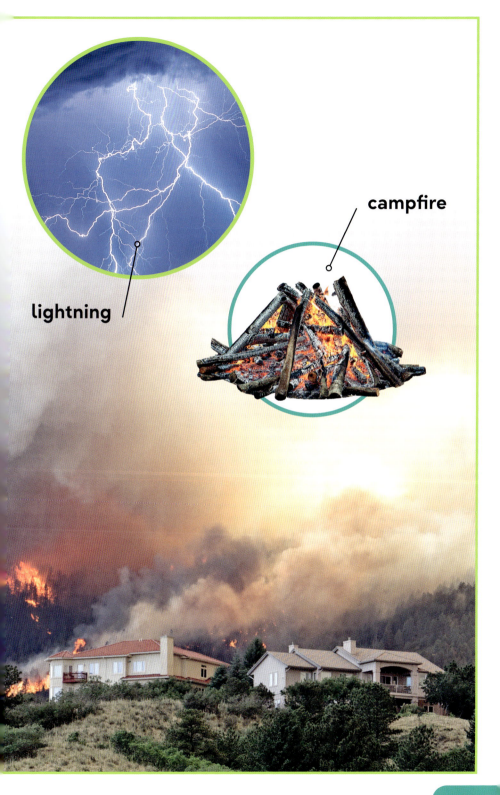

tile roof

stucco

To limit fire damage, many buildings in fire-prone areas are made of stucco, stone, or brick. They have tile roofs. These fire-resistant materials help the buildings withstand wildfires.

Good Advice
If authorities tell people to evacuate their homes because of a wildfire, they should leave immediately.

Driveways and paver patios can also help prevent fire damage. They don't burn like trees and shrubs do. They can be used to create a buffer zone around a building. If the fire doesn't cross the zone, it can't reach the building.

There are many kinds of natural disasters. Tornadoes and earthquakes can flatten a home. Hurricanes, floods, and tsunamis can fill homes with water or wash them away. Blizzards can cave in roofs, and wildfires can burn houses to the ground. Each of these disasters poses a risk.

People can't stop natural disasters from happening. But they can prepare for them. Making strong buildings is one way to do that.

Strong buildings help keep people safe. They provide shelter. They are a good place to be when nature has a bad day.

Glossary

Bedrock
Solid rock that lies under soil

Blizzard
A long, heavy snowstorm

Debris
The remains of something that has been destroyed

Earthquake
A shaking or movement of part of Earth's surface

Evacuate
To move or take away from a dangerous place

Flood
A great flow of water that spreads over land

Foundation
The structure that provides support at the bottom of a building

Hurricane
A powerful storm with heavy rains and winds of at least 74 miles per hour (119 kph)

Laminated
Made of thin layers stuck together

Natural Disaster
A sudden and terrible event in nature that usually results in serious damage

Pendulum
A hanging weight that swings back and forth

Perimeter
The outer edge of a shape or area

Resistant
Able to prevent something or keep something away

Stilts
Thin poles that raise and support a building

Storm surge
A dangerous, quick rise in sea level that often occurs during a hurricane

Stucco
A plaster-like material used to cover walls inside or outside a home

Tornado
Destructive winds from a funnel-shaped cloud that moves in a narrow path

Tsunami
A giant wave on the ocean caused by an underwater earthquake or volcanic eruption

Wildfire
A large, destructive fire that spreads quickly and can be hard to control

Index

amphibious houses 30–31

bedrock 16

blizzards 36–39, 44

campfires 40, 41

climate change 22

concrete 12, 16, 24, 27, 31

dome-shaped buildings 11, 24–25, 38–39

earthquakes 14–21, 33, 44

evacuation 35, 43

fires 40–43, 44

floating buildings 30–31

floods 22, 25, 28–35, 44

foundation 16, 17

hurricanes 22–28, 44

igloos 39

laminated glass 26

lightning 40, 41

pendulum 20, 21

plywood 12

roofs 36, 42

round buildings 11

safe rooms 13

safety 8, 33

skyscrapers 15–21

snow 36–39

spiderwebs 19

square buildings 12

steel
    earthquakes 16, 18, 19
    floods 31
    hurricanes 24
    tornadoes 12, 13

stilts 29

storm surge 22, 25, 28

stucco 42

tile roof 42

tornadoes 8–13, 44

tsunamis 32–35, 44

ultra-high performance concrete (UHPC) 27

waves 33

wildfires 40–43, 44

windows 26

winds
    blizzards 36
    dome-shaped homes 11, 24
    hurricanes 22, 24, 26
    skyscrapers 20
    tornadoes 8, 10, 13

Quiz

Answer the questions to see what you have learned. Check your answers in the key below.

1. Which building shape is the most resistant to tornadoes?
2. True or False: Some buildings are earthquake proof.
3. What helps keep Taipei 101 standing during strong winds?
4. What kind of natural disaster was the Eye of the Storm house built to withstand?
5. Name two ways to protect homes from floods.
6. True or False: A beach is a good place to find shelter during a tsunami.
7. Why do homes need strong roofs to survive a blizzard?
8. What are three materials often used to build homes in wildfire-prone areas?

1. A dome 2. False 3. A giant pendulum 4. A hurricane
5. Build homes on stilts or make homes that float 6. False
7. Snow is very heavy 8. Stucco, stone, and brick